W9-AHW-914

MAJESTIC
INDIA

MAJESTIC
INDIA

Text and photography by
Tarun Chopra

Copyright © 1998, 1996 Tarun Chopra and Local Colour Limited, Hong Kong.

Revised edition 1998.

The moral rights of the author has been asserted.

All rights reserved. Without limiting the rights under copyright reserved above, no part of this publication may be reproduced, stored, or introduced into a retrieval system, or transmitted, in any form, or by any means (electronic, mechanical, photocopying, recording or otherwise), without the prior written permission of both the copyright holder and the above publisher of the book.

A CIP catalogue record for this is available from the British Library.

Title Page: *The Taj Mahal is the monumental tomb built by the great Mughal emperor, Shah Jahan, in tribute to his wife Mumtaz Mahal. Beside the tomb are two buildings: a mosque on the west side and a jawab on the east.*

Right: *Turbans in India were once worn by king and servant alike. Each region, state and community has its own unique way of fashioning yards of colourful fabric into complex turbans. In Rajasthan turbans in of many vibrant hues are still worn.*

Photography, text and captions: Tarun Chopra
Front cover: Fredrik Arvidsson

Editor: John Oliver
Design: Harvey Symons

ISBN 962-217-550-3

Printed in Hong Kong

India is a land of great geographical diversity, with towering snow-covered mountain ranges, lush forests, endless coasts and arid deserts. This diversity has fostered a unique cultural heritage in the clothing, food, literature, festivals and artistic traditions of each region.

Rajasthan is called the Land of Kings. It is a region of rolling sand dunes and desert tracks, austere forts and romantic palaces. Against the monochromatic desert landscape the people wear exuberant brightly-coloured costumes embroidered with animal, bird and flower patterns.

Peninsular India is fringed by the beautiful beaches of Goa and Kerala to the west, and Madras and Puri to the east. The long welcoming coastline has brought trade and travellers to the shores of India for centuries. While there are many thriving commercial cities along the sea, many beaches remain picturesque, with fishing boats, swaying palm trees, and golden sands.

11

This country of many cultures, religions and races is also a country of great youth; today almost half of India's 900 million people are below the age of 15.

The majority of India's population is Hindu, however Muslims, Sikhs, Christians, Jains, Zoroastrians, Buddhists and a small community of Jews constitute the rest of Indian society.

INTRODUCTION

India has attracted travellers for thousands of years. Among the first to venture to this land were the Aryans, or Indo-Europeans, of Central Asia, from the region around the Caspian Sea. They settled along the Indus river and its tributaries as far back as 3,000 BC. As their numbers increased, some of them were forced into migration. They eventually re-established themselves in the Doab region, which lies between the Yamuna and Ganges rivers. Evidence of their lifestyles was unearthed by archaeologists who found numerous artefacts of significance. The discovery of iron and copper enabled these nomadic tribes to develop permanent homes all across northern and central India.

With permanency, these nascent societies soon evolved manageable forms of local government and administration. They elected an administrator who bore the title 'raja'. His task was to oversee the safety of the village from attacks by other tribes, to maintain law and order, and to ensure that the agricultural revenue due to the state was duly received. The raja was supported by a Council of Ministers who were each accountable to local assemblies called the Sabha and Samiti. These bodies were the watchdogs of society and were empowered to even overthrow the raja if his style of governance did not meet with their approval, or if it adversely affected the interests of the village. It was in these times that the first tentative roots of democracy took hold in India. Over the centuries, this system became more firmly entrenched, and today's democratic government is merely an extension of an ancient Indian tradition.

As trade grew in the villages along the Ganges, the people within each society came to be recognised by their principal occupation. Some were involved in the teaching and dissemination of knowledge contained in the religious scriptures, others were traders and small scale manufacturers, and yet another section of society performed the menial tasks of daily living. Some sociologists are convinced that the caste system sprang from this division of labour. This four-fold division of society, occasionally referred to as varna, was based on the colour of a person's skin, which was also a factor in deciding what jobs would be allocated to him within the hierarchy. Accordingly, three castes were initially established:

(i) Brahmins, tall and fair-skinned with sharp features, were accorded the duties of teachers.

(ii) Kshatriyas (warriors) bore the responsibility of maintaining law and order within the village, and had to provide protection against invaders.

(iii) Vaishyas, the dark-skinned, were assigned menial tasks and were also merchants in society.

Gradually, a fourth class was added to the list as the social structure grew increasingly complex. The Sudras performed tasks the Vaishyas would not undertake to do, such as cleaning and meeting the sanitary needs of the village. They lived on the outskirts of society, often along the village boundaries. It is believed that initially the caste system was very fluid, enabling free movement from one level to another, until an increasingly complicated social administration set out to control this flexibility by decreeing that birth and heredity alone would determine one's caste. Thus, India's class differences would from this point onwards be immutably established.

The Brahmins were quick to provide intellectual justification for the caste system by quoting from the Vedas, the basic Hindu scriptures: from the mouth of Brahma (one of the gods in the Hindu trinity—Trimurti—Brahma represents creation) came the Brahmins, whose job it was to preach; from the arms came the Kshatriyas, whose job it was to defend the society; from the loins came the Vaishyas, whose job it was to do business; and from the feet came the Sudras, whose job it was to carry the weight of the whole society by performing manual labour like skinning dead animals, cleaning up filth and keeping the village neat and tidy.

By about 600 BC the caste system was irrevocably fixed, with the Brahmins becoming key advisers to the government, the Kshatriyas and Vaishyas managing trade and manufacture, and the Sudras relegated to the fringes of society. But this social order proved inadequate with the changes in the socio-economic scenario, especially in north India. Out of this deficiency, therefore, sprang two new religions — Jainism and Buddhism — which promised equality and offered the hope of better living conditions through increased social mobility for all classes of society.

In time land ownership became common, which further divided society. This new conflict justified the establishment of an organised central power which gave rise to prominent kingdoms along the middle reaches of the Ganges around the 5th century BC. By the 6th century BC, the kingdom of Magadha emerged as the dominant power in the region. During the 3rd century BC, the mighty Emperor Ashoka was responsible for the spread of the Mauryan empire, which succeeded Magadha. Following his conversion to Buddhism after the Kalinga war of 260 BC, Ashoka encouraged the practice of non-violence and renunciation, and preached the Buddha's message of peace and harmony throughout the land. During the Mauryan empire Ashoka erected stone pillars, many surmounted with the lion capital which was later adopted as the emblem of the Republic of India. His rock inscriptions not only give details of his reign but also dictate civil and personal laws.

Emperor Ashoka was a pioneer in envisaging a nation-state, and the edicts of his administration are found as far away as Afghanistan, Orissa and the Deccan. He divided his empire into four zones so that administration and communication could be facilitated. The system of taxation that he developed—based on a detailed study of land and agriculture—is continued, to some degree, even today.

In 326 BC, Alexander the Great invaded northwest India and defeated Porus, whose kingdom stretched along the banks of the Beas river, a tributary of the Indus. Unlike his Islamic successors, Alexander did not venture any further. Alexander's influence brought to bear upon Indian art, architecture and philosophy a Grecian style, which was further reinforced by King Meander (155—130 BC), who expanded the Indo-Greek Kingdom of Bactria to include part of the Punjab. For almost 1,000 years, Taxila (in present-day Pakistan) remained an important religious, commercial and artistic centre. During the 1st century, the Kushan empire spanned from Peshawar, in the extreme northwest, to Benaras on the Ganges, with centres also at Gandhara and Mathura. The Buddhist art of this period was heavily influenced by the Greeks. Much of this art from around Peshawar and the Swat Valley can be seen today in museums at Chandigarh and New Delhi.

However, the classical age in the evolution of Indian civilization blossomed for over two centuries (320—540) under the imperial Gupta dynasty. The dynasty ruled northern and central India, with capitals at Ujjain, and later Ayodhya. Some of the earliest surviving temples in India—at Sanchi and Nachna—originate from this period. There was a strong Hindu revival while official recognition of Buddhist monasteries continued. The Jain trading community also prospered. Besides art and architecture, the Gupta rule left a lasting impression on the literature and philosophy of India. Kalidas' famous play, 'Shakuntala', and the Indian treatise on love-making chronicled in the 'Kamasutra', were written during the Gupta period. Many outstanding contributions to metallurgy, mathematics and the sciences, including the concept of 'zero', also originated during this time. The astronomer Aryabhatta conceived the theory that the earth orbited around the sun, although his views were largely ignored. An iron pillar—now erected in Delhi—inscribed with the name of Chandra Gupta II (373—414), stands under open skies without a trace of rust, in mute testimony of the advanced metallurgical practices of the day.

Under the later Guptas, orthodox Hinduism was once again asserted, often encouraged by the rulers against the many sects that had emerged. This led to religious intolerance and hostilities, and the peaceful coexistence between Buddhists and Brahmins, recounted in the memoirs of the 5th-century Chinese traveller, Fa Hsien, slowly disintegrated.

With this breakdown in tolerance, the caste system once again took hold and this time its re-emergence was stronger than ever before. A group of people known as 'Untouchables' were differentiated from even the lowest caste. They were held as outcastes of society and suffered untold privations and affronts to their safety and personal dignity. Even the sight of them was deemed sufficient to pollute the upper castes. The rigidity of the caste system, and the many injustices against the Untouchables, continued well into Independence. The government today still faces the task of eradicating this evil.

Following the Guptas came many smaller dynasties, including the Prathiharas. By this time India had undergone many significant changes. Cardinal amongst them was the decline in external and internal trade which supplemented, to a great degree, the agricultural revenue of the entire land. With this came a weighty ruralisation of the economy. This turn of events caused the currency in circulation to de-value against the consequent localisation of economic and administrative units since the states were unable to pay the salaries of the civil and defence officials. Furthermore, charitable grants to temples and to the Brahmins had to be curbed. The Indian economy came to be defined as 'agrarian' both for the state as well as for the individual, which, to all intents and purposes, is what it is today. In the years that followed the Gupta period significant attention was paid to the development of agriculture. As far back as the reign of Harsha (605—647), who ruled northern India from Kanauj, the considerable progress in agriculture was appreciated by the Chinese traveller, Hiuen Tsang, who made extensive notes during his travels. Hiuen Tsang was particularly impressed by the spread of Buddhism and Nalanda university, which had 4,000 students enrolled. The university library housed all the major texts of Buddhist philosophy and, when it was the object of wanton arson by the Turks in the 12th century, it is said that the manuscripts took three months to burn completely.

Harsha was murdered by his minister in 647. This led to the fragmentation of northern India into a number of petty kingdoms, the rulers of which were constantly at war with each other. In the absence of a central controlling body, science and culture made little advancement. In southern India, other kingdoms rose and fell. The Buddhist kingdom of Andhra had its capital at Amaravati, near the delta of the Krishna and Godavari rivers. Between the Deccan and the west coast a series of Buddhist caves were excavated. The great caves of Ajanta are the most famous examples, with their prayer and monastic halls adorned with some of the finest murals of any civilization.

One of the early dynasties in southern India was the Chalukyas, who built the great capitals and temples at Badami, Aihole and Pattadakal. To the southeast, the Pallava kings ruled with their capital at Kanchipuram, while to the north, along the Western Ghats and the Deccan, the Rastrakutas governed, leaving the monumental rock-cut temples of Elephanta, near Bombay, and Ellora.

An even more influential dynasty ruled present-day Tamil Nadu from the 10th century onwards. The Cholas of the 10th and 11th centuries were believers in Shiva, the powerful Hindu god of destruction, and became important patrons of temple architecture. The great temples of Chidambaram and Thanjavur in south India, and the Hindu influence in temples as far east as Bali and Cambodia, can be traced to the Chola period. Under their patronage, bronze sculpture also flourished.

As a result of northern domination on Indian culture, the contribution of the south has been largely overlooked. This is unfortunate since the fields of art and architecture, and the schools of Indian thought and philosophy which emerged from the thinking of the south, have a distinct influence and flavour.

RELIGION AND SOCIETY IN INDIA

Anyone who wishes to comprehend Indian society has to take cognizance of the important role religion plays in every aspect of life on the subcontinent. All the world's major religions are represented here: Hinduism, Islam, Christianity, Buddhism, Jainism, Sikhism, Zoroastrianism and Judaism. Besides these, a variety of sects determine the religious sentiments of the people. No wonder nothing can describe this country more aptly than the title, 'a museum of religions'. The influence of these various religions over centuries has resulted in a great deal of religious tolerance and secularism. While Europe underwent the Reformation, which divided the State and religion, India moved more definitely to accommodate all religions on par with Hinduism, the dominant religion in the country.

Hinduism

To define the underlying tenets of Hinduism would be a most arduous task for many. There is no basic philosophy that describes the beliefs of the majority of India's people. Many different schools of thought, each no less important than the other, give direction and inspiration. The Rig Veda, Upanishads or Bhagwad Gita can each be described as the sacred text of the Hindus without any infringement on the authenticity of the statement. Even if the sacred texts are dispensed with it is possible to define Hinduism by one's own beliefs and claim to be a good, practising member of the faith. Unlike Christianity or Islam, where one's approach is more definitely controlled by the precepts set out in religious texts and edicts, Hinduism can be described more as a 'way of life'. Therefore, it is not uncommon to have Hindus describe their worship in a number of heterogeneous ways. Some will pledge belief in Vishnu or Shiva, or any other god or goddess of the Hindu pantheon, or in none at all! Others will express their faith in sacrificial rituals or undertake a long pilgrimage. This freedom to worship as many deities as there are has conferred upon Hindus a high level of tolerance for other religions. Nowhere is this more evident than in the sculptures of the myriad gods and goddesses on temple walls, depicting the many moods and themes of the Hindu pantheon.

To understand Hinduism it is important to appreciate profound concepts of 'ultimate reality' at one end of the scale and the worship of spirits and animals at the other. Monism and pluralism are inextricably linked. It was pluralism that enabled Hinduism to withstand the influence of foreign invading armies. Hinduism readily accepted the tenets of other faiths, which probably kept it as buoyant as ever when external influences dominated the land. Today, not unnaturally, temple, church and mosque coexist in peaceful communion even in the smallest and remotest town or village in the country.

Hindu Festivals and Ceremonies

The Hindu festivals and ceremonies are so many that someone once remarked that there is a festival for every day in the year. The festivals are occasions to worship and honour not just gods, goddesses or local heroes but also the sun, moon, stars and planets. On these occasions the town comes alive with gaily decorated bazaars and local entertainment. The town also witnesses the arrival of numerous sadhus, or wandering hermits, who are easily recognised by their saffron robes and bodies smeared with ash and sandalwood paste. They not only lend their presence to the festivities but also chant hymns or religious songs from the Vedas or other ancient Hindu scriptures. Characteristic of them, nobody knows where the sadhus come from or where they live — the Himalayas or in mountain caves perhaps — and they just as mysteriously disappear when the day is done.

Some Basic Hindu Religious Texts

The principal Hindu texts are the Vedas and the Upanishads. The Vedas are hymns or songs of praise which are at the heart of all Hindu teachings. Probably composed between 1,600 and 1,500 BC, they celebrate the oneness of divine principle (with tolerance of all religions) and man's union with Nature. This very accurately encompasses the scale of belief from pluralism to monism. The Vedas further decreed that ritualistic worship was essential to absolve sin and ensure purification of the sinner. This evolved into the practice of lighting a fire or offering sacrifices called yagnas before the start of a ceremony. In time, these rituals gave undue importance to the Brahmins, or priestly class, who conducted them. Moreover, the ceremony gained stature over the vedic teachings, where performance of rituals was considered sufficient to purify.

The Upanishads evolved to stem the downward trend in Hinduism. They encapsulated dialogues between teacher and disciple or guru and shishya. The monistic temper of the Vedas was stressed, where reality—the essence of our existence, or the absolute—was called Atman and could be attained not by reason but by intuition. It is probably this belief that has governed the Hindu way of thinking and behaving. In all walks of life, and under any circumstances, intuition takes precedence over logic, and reason is relegated to a lesser place in everyday life.

Without mention of the Bhagwad Gita, or the 'Song of God', the most popular vedic text, this review of Hindu religious texts would be incomplete. The epic Mahabharata, which contains the Gita, shows strong links with the Upanishads. It is the story of the five Pandava brothers, who lost their kingdom to their cousins, the Kauravas. On the eve of a crucial battle for dominance, Arjuna, the Pandava leader, enters into a discourse with Krishna, an incarnation of Lord Vishnu. Krishna talks about the importance of duty, the immortality of the soul, abandonment of worldly attachments and also of the necessity to dedicate the fruit of one's work to the divine. This is the essence of the teachings of the Gita.

No less important is the way to self-realization or the divine. Three paths have to be traversed — the path of jnana (knowledge), the path of bhakti (devotion and love) and the path of karma (work). These represent the intellectual, emotional and practical aspects of every human being. Yoga is believed to awaken the soul and set it forth on the course of self-realization.

Hindu Mythology

A veritable storehouse of myths, Indian religious literature explains complex philosophical precepts through simple stories that even the illiterate can comprehend. Many of them are contained in the two great epics, the Mahabharata and the Ramayana. The Ramayana is the story of Rama's 14-year banishment to the jungle by his scheming stepmother and his life in exile with his brother, Lakshman, and his wife, Sita. Sita's kidnapping by Ravana, the demon-king of Lanka, and her eventual rescue by Hanuman, the monkey-devotee of Rama, are all woven into this engrossing tale. Rama stands for the perfect man — faultless as king, brother, husband and son. Legends woven into these and other works have been passed down orally from one generation to the next. Religious festivals, fairs and rituals keep these myths alive, and there is never an occasion that does not offer an opportunity to retell the old stories.

Gods of the Hindu Pantheon

There is no single 'Jesus Christ' or 'Prophet Mohammed' that the Hindus can look to for divine guidance and inspiration. There are many gods and goddesses, epitomizing different virtues or forces of Nature. Among them, the most fundamental to Hinduism, is the trinity of Brahma, Vishnu and Shiva — creator, preserver and destroyer.

Brahma, the creator, has four heads which correspond to the four main directions of the compass. As he is formless, he finds no place in temples, though most invocations are addressed to him. Vishnu, as preserver, guides the cycle of birth and rebirth, and is supposed to have been, in various incarnations, Rama and Krishna. Vishnu is married to Lakshmi, the goddess of wealth and prosperity.

Shiva, being the destroyer, has for his partner Shakti (energy), who is known in her benign and terrible aspects as Parvati and Kali, respectively. Shiva, like Vishnu, has many incarnations, or avatars, not all of which are terrifying.

Mention must also be made of Krishna, whose teachings are embodied in the Bhagwad Gita as Arjuna's friend, philosopher and guide. He is considered the eighth avatar of Vishnu and appears as a warrior in the Mahabharata. This most human of gods is remembered for his playful escapades with gopis, or young milkmaids, in his youth. Later in life, Radha's yearning for Lord Krishna is seen as a symbol of the union of the human spirit with the divine.

The many Hindu gods and goddesses are particularly appealing as they are not above human fallibility; something easily recognised by all of us.

The Fundamentals of Hinduism

Hinduism is based on philosophical traditions that are an amalgamation of the many influences it was subjected to in the past. Accordingly, its basic tenets are:

The goals of Hinduism: The ultimate aim of all mortals is moksha, or release from the cycle of existence—birth and rebirth. It can be attained in a number of ways.

Karma and rebirth: Hinduism is based on the theory that the soul survives the body after death. All human beings are subject to the cycle of birth and rebirth, depending on the law of karma or deeds in the previous life. The quality of life in the next birth is determined by the deeds performed in one's previous lives — good deeds reap the harvest of a better life and bad deeds are the cause for suffering in subsequent rebirths.

Purposes of life: Besides moksha, life has three major goals. Kama (pleasure), artha (prosperity and fame) and, highest of the three, dharma (truth and righteousness).

Four stages of life: A Hindu's life is divided into four stages of being: student (brahmacharya), householder (grihastha), detachment from worldly goods (vanaprastha) and renunciation, which is the state of spiritual readiness for liberation or moksha.

The four castes: Caste is believed to be determined by one's actions or karma in a previous birth. There are four castes in Indian society: Brahmins, Kshatriyas, Vaishyas and Sudras. One of the means of finding release from the cycle of existence is by yoga, or inner control, which through meditation and exercise shepherds the body and mind into recognition of one's inner strength. 'Self-recognition' is the only means by which peace can be achieved and the passions of the spirit finally quelled. Yoga is essentially practised under the guidance of a guru or spiritual leader.

The Transformation of Hinduism in Modern Times

Hinduism, instead of remaining static, has changed over the years by absorbing external influences, trends and innovations, particularly from the West. Attitudes such as liberalism, humanism, technological advances and a scientific temper have been smoothly incorporated, which more than exemplifies the ability of Hinduism to adopt new ideas and adapt itself in the face of change.

However, this new impact led to the upsurge of both the revivalist and modernist movements. While, on the one hand, there was an effort to shut out all change, on the other, there was a concerted bid to introduce a new way of thinking. Though isolated cases of sati, or bride burning, occurred in Rajasthan in western India, concurrently social reforms like widow remarriage, the education of women and equality of women were also introduced. What this new influence did was primarily to allow Hinduism to be subjected to scrutiny. This in turn determined which elements of the religion needed to be preserved and encouraged and which practices were outmoded and were best rejected. The result of this examination was that the 'modernity of tradition', as it was called, received much support and led to the conflict much in evidence today at all levels of Hindu society, where the old and the new are locked into inherent contradiction.

The Offshoots of Hinduism—Buddhism and Jainism

The original spirit of Hinduism got lost somewhere along the way, largely because the predominance of ritualism and the rigid caste system. This was sought to be rectified by the rise of two new religions in the 6th century BC — Buddhism and Jainism.

Buddhism

Of the two offshoots of Hinduism, Buddhism has been more successful, both in India and abroad. It has a wide following particularly in China, Japan and Southeast Asia and is also gaining popularity elsewhere in the world.

Buddhism works on two basic principles: the 'law of impermanence' states that everything is subject to change, though some things may last longer than others; the 'law of causation' states that nothing happens purely by chance. The law of karma follows from this. Gautam Buddha explained his dharma, or philosophy, in his sermon of the 'Middle Way'. He set out that abstinence and denial of everything as real was the path that ultimately led to the realisation of the 'Four Noble Truths': suffering is the universal destiny of humanity; its main cause lies in desire and yearning; suffering can be prevented and overcome; and, lastly, that the eradication of desires can lead to the cessation of suffering (dukkha). To achieve these goals, self-control and the need to perfect oneself are essential. Compliance with these tenets, the Buddha preached, is the only path to nirvana or the extinction of all that hinders enlightenment or clear sight. It is possible to see the strong lines of similarity between the basic beliefs of Buddhism and those of Hinduism. It is no wonder, therefore, that Hindus are generally very accepting of this religion.

Jainism

Conquering one's weakness through renunciation of worldly desires leads to perfection—this is the underlying philosophy of Jainism. Ideally, there should be total abstinence and asceticism as practised by the Jinas and Tirthankaras, the saints revered more than the gods by the Jains. Though the Hindu pantheon finds acceptance in this faith, the concept of 'God' is not central to Jainism.

Mahavira, the 'Great Hero', preached the Jaina philosophy around the time Buddhism began. Both religions were opposed to the corruption in interpreting Hinduism and questioned some of its practices like casteism, which categorises human beings by their birth. As Jainism has a lot in common with its mother religion, Hinduism, Jains find wide acceptance in India. Its particular genius lies in its emphasis on equal kindness toward all living creatures.

Islam

The Arabs first brought Islam to India in the early 8th century, but it was not until the 12th century that it became a force to reckon with. Unlike Buddhism, Jainism and Sikhism, which sprung up as offshoots of Hinduism and share much in common, the concept and customs of Islam are far removed from Hinduism. This led to a series of conflicts between the two communities before conciliation took place.

Differences between Hinduism and Islam

The Quran, propounded by Prophet Mohammed, is the foundation on which Islam rests.

Hinduism, on the other hand, is pluralistic and does not have any single scripture specific to its teachings. This probably explains why Islam is cohesive and homogenous whilst the precepts of Hinduism advocate proper behaviour with emphasis on self-denial and abstinence. Furthermore, Islam encourages uncluttered living whilst Hinduism has no such rigid injunction. Nothing is more strikingly different than their forms of worship. Islam abhors idol worship, yet the idol is central to Hindu worship and reverence. This concept has also influenced the architecture of temples and mosques, in which the former always has an inner sanctum where the idol is enshrined.

These differences were the source of initial conflict when Islam was first introduced in India. But under the rule of the great Mughal emperor Akbar, in the 16th century, much adjustment and conciliation took place. Over the years, Islam became integrated into Indian culture.

Christianity

Opinion is divided as to the date of the advent of Christianity in India. Some maintain that it is as old as St. Thomas, one of Christ's apostles, who is said to have spent some years near Madras in south India until his death. Others say that the first missionary to visit this country was St. Bartholomew.

Whatever, Christian missionary activity got truly started under the guidance of St. Francis Xavier, whose tomb in Goa is today a centre of pilgrimage for thousands of Christians. He arrived in 1542 and was succeeded by missionaries from Germany, Denmark, Holland and, after the British conquest, even the Anglican Church.

Much of the modern attitude of India can be attributed to the role of Christianity in its development. Despite accusations by Hindu conservatives that the missionaries were carrying out conversions, they were primarily engaged in social improvement by education and social reform. Even remote areas in the hills and backward districts enjoyed the presence of schools, and women and tribes people were helped enormously by their influence. With the establishment of educational centres came the need for printing presses, though it was believed that they were set up mainly to spread the 'message' of faith and goodwill. So impressed was Mahatma Gandhi, and other intellectuals, with the work of the missionaries that he incorporated the teachings of Jesus Christ into the efforts to free India from British rule.

Today the Christians in India number 30 million and are not confrontational in their attitude towards other communities.

Judaism

The Jewish community, which numbered about 30,000 when India declared Independence in 1947, has shrunk considerably in recent years with most young Jews opting to leave for their homeland in Israel or to head for other countries. The two main communities which continue to live here are the Cochin Jews of Kerala in the south and the Bene Israel on the west coast, near Bombay.

Sikhism

The Sikh religion emerged during the late 15th and early 16th century in Punjab in north India. Guru Nanak, its founder, was unhappy with the rituals and rigid caste system of

Hindu practice which segregated human beings according to birth. To remove this stifling influence, he visited many places within India on pilgrimage and even went to Mecca with a Muslim companion. After his death, his teachings were collected and later incorporated in the Adi Granth (or 'Guru Granth Sahib'), the holy book of the Sikhs.

Sikhism propounds faith in one God and, as a protection against the caste system, imposes the surname 'Singh' uniformly on everyone. Apart from this, many Sikh practices are common to Hindus. Inter-marriages between them are also common, which has brought the two communities somewhat closer. This is especially relevant since the 1980s witnessed a rise in terrorism by Sikh fundamentalists, who do not enjoy the support of the Sikh majority. By and large, the Sikh community observes the tenets expressed in their holy book, which is founded on Hindu and Muslim beliefs.

Religion in Contemporary India

Though India has made immense progress in science and technology, religion still holds a prominent place in contemporary India. Almost every major conflict has been linked to religion, more than even class differences and economic exploitation. Despite the rising force of fundamentalism, credit is due to the Indian state that has maintained the secular face of the nation.

The Coming of the Muslims

Pre-Independence India has been divided rather arbitrarily, for convenience it would seem, into three periods: the Vedic age, up to the 12th century, is called the 'Hindu period'; 1200 to 1707 is known as the 'Muslim period'; while the 'British period' falls between 1707 and 1947.

Within 100 years of the Muslim Prophet's death in 632, Arab raiders attacked the north-west frontier in the hope of plundering and amassing India's famed riches. They plundered the temples of Mathura, Kanauj and Somnathpur of hidden stores of gold and silver. These sorties, more for loot than expansion, were organised by Mahmud Gazni.

Almost two centuries later, a fresh horde of invaders, this time led by Mohammed Ghori, made their presence felt. Once again, they were from Central Asia, and again their target was north India. But this time they came to settle down and make this land their home. They had overran the northern half of the subcontinent by the first quarter of the 13th century. They created a new state with Delhi as their capital and Islam as the official religion. After Mohammed Ghori's death, Qutub-ud-Din Aibak declared himself 'Sultan of Delhi'. He was also responsible for the basic edicts of the sultanate which continued for the next three centuries. Other dynasties followed: the Tughluqs (1320—1413), the Sayyids (1414—14 51), and the Lodis (1451—1526).

During the first five centuries of their rule in India, the Muslims played a significant role in the development of art, architecture and culture. New building styles—arches, minarets and the round domes on rectangular bases—were imported from the Middle East. The Qutub Minar is a fine example of the architecture of Central Asia which Qutub-ud-Din Aibak introduced in India. But an entirely different style of construction evolved in areas not under Muslim domination. The great sculptures of the temples of Khajuraho in Madhya Pradesh, Konark in Orissa, Madurai, Rameshwaram and Thanjavur in the south, have a divine and often sensuous symbolism that was endemic of the Hindus of that period.

During the Tughluq rule, the Hindu kingdom of Vijayanagar and the Muslim realm of Bahamani, towards the south, were caught up in incessant battle—a common enough scene in the rest of India at that time. However, this one led to the disintegration of the Delhi Sultanate in the latter half of the 13th century, which the secessionist forces had increasingly weakened. However, both the Vijayanagar and Bahamani kingdoms left a legacy of fine monuments, although few, sadly, survived the ravages of battle. The weakened dynasty was easy prey for Babur, a descendant of Timur and Genghis Khan, who was to become the first Mughal emperor. Ibrahim Lodi's forces were routed in the battle of Panipat near Delhi in 1526 by Babur and his conquering invaders.

THE GREAT MUGHALS

Zahir-ud-Din Mohammed Babur

Babur founded the Mughal empire in India and stretched its suzerainty as far as the Deccan. He had the famous Koh-i-Noor diamond in his possession. He died, aged forty-seven, in Agra, but was buried in his garden in Kabul, according to his last wishes. His work, the 'Babur Nama', initiated the royal tradition of writing autobiographies among his successors.

Humayun

Humayun inherited a vast though unstable empire which covered much of northern India and was constantly threatened by the Rajputs under Rana Sanga of Chittor and the Afghans. He was forced to flee to Persia in 1540 after his defeat by Sher Shah, who succeeded him.

In 1555, Humayun returned with an army. Notwithstanding, he was able to rule for only six months before falling to his death from a staircase in the Purana Qila fort. A historian once said about the ineffectual ruler, 'Humayan tumbled through life and tumbled out of it.'

Sher Shah and Islam Shah

Sher Khan, an ambitious Afghan chief from Bihar, has the unique status of being the only non-Mughal who dared lead the Mughal empire. Sher Shah ruled only for five years, followed by an uncertain period under his son, Islam Shah. This fifteen-year break in the dynasty made a wandering exile of the rightful ruler. Sher Khan, who had by then adopted the name Sher Shah, made many lasting contributions, such as developing trunk roads, and many of his administrative reforms were further developed during Akbar's reign.

Akbar the Great

Akbar was, in a sense, the true founder of the Mughal empire, as he consolidated the gains of his grandfather, Babur. He realised that in order to strengthen his empire, which now covered both north and south India, he needed the support of local chieftains. Instead of antagonising them by a policy of aggrandizement, he decided on a policy of reconciliation.

The Rajput princes, who were then his greatest challenge, were propitiated by offers of the highest imperial offices and by marriages with Mughal daughters. Akbar was able to reduce every opposition group to a whisper. Because he had married into respected Hindu families by taking several Rajput wives, his Muslim cousins as well as his Hindu in-laws had to practise religious toleration, a cause he firmly believed in. Akbar was the first truly secular leader of modern India who recognised the power of religion and the importance of amity between communities for the strength and survival of the national fabric.

Although illiterate, Akbar was an avid patron of the arts. He had great appreciation for painting, literature and music. Works in Latin, Sanskrit and Turkish were translated under his aegis and royal artists illustrated his manuscripts. He invited Christian (Jesuits from Goa, which was colonised by the Portuguese), Hindu, Jain, Jewish and Parsi scholars for religious discussions. He created a new world religion, Din-i-Elahi. Akbar is remembered in history because he managed to hold a vast empire together by inspiring respect for all religions. Akbar was childless for a long time, despite his harem of 300 wives, which made him a very unhappy man until at last his Hindu wife, Jodha Bai, bore him a son, Salim, who later succeeded him to the throne as Jahangir.

Akbar built the city of Fatehpur Sikri, near Agra, in dedication to the mystic saint, Shaikh Salim Chishti, who predicted the birth of this son. Akbar's tomb at Sikandra, eight kilometres from Agra, was built to a plan he approved before his death in 1605.

Jahangir

Jahangir was too fond of wine and women to make any lasting conquests or contributions, though he did consolidate parts of central India. He could afford to lead a dissipated life because Akbar, his father, had left him a large and stable empire. The emperor's drinking was such an open secret that Thomas Roe, the British ambassador who visited the royal court, presented him with bottles of liquor. Nepotism and political intrigue became common. His wife, Nur Jahan, was well known for her beauty and machinations in the affairs of the court.

As Jahangir's distractions made it increasingly difficult for him to attend to his courtly duties, his son, Shah Jahan, took over and finally became his successor against powerful opposition from within the family.

Shah Jahan

For more than anything else, Shah Jahan is remembered for his great contributions to architecture. He moved his capital from Agra to Delhi in 1648 and built the Red Fort and the Jama Masjid (Friday Mosque) there. He personally supervised the planning and construction of these monuments. This is why he is called the 'great builder' of the Mughal empire.

He was deeply in love with Mumtaz Mahal, the queen closest to him, and was grief stricken when she passed away giving birth to her fourteenth child. As a monument to their love, he built the exquisite Taj Mahal, one of the great wonders of the world. He lies there, buried next to her.

Shah Jahan was also interested in jewellery. He created the beautiful Peacock Throne, which was studded with diamonds, rubies and pearls and weighed a ton in gold. However, all these extravagances drained the royal treasury and indirectly created a bitter struggle for power among his brothers. Though he had wanted his son, Dara Shikoh, to succeed him, it was his wily third son, Aurangzeb, who came to the throne and kept Shah Jahan imprisoned in the Agra Fort until his death in 1666.

Aurangzeb

Aurangzeb's religious bigotry and unfair policies alienated the Hindu populace and led him into unnecessary confrontations with powerful Hindus like the formidable Marathas, led by Shivaji. He frittered away his energies in domestic wars and this led to the inexorable deterioration of the Mughal empire.

Once again India was too weak and divided to resist foreign aggression. First came Nadir Shah of Persia, in 1738, who plundered Delhi for two months and looted the city of the Peacock Throne and other precious possessions, which he took away in caravans borne by camels and elephants. By the second half of the 18th century, the British and Europeans had begun to absorb small kingdoms into the areas they administered while many rulers were deeply and bitterly divided and could offer little resistance to the conquering armies.

THE BRITISH IN INDIA

Vasco da Gama's visit to India in 1498 marked the beginning of the West's interest in India. Over the years this led to the setting up of British, French, Dutch and Portuguese trading companies which had initially established their presence in the land with 'factories' (more precisely warehouses) of cotton, spices, silks, muslin and precious stones around the port towns. These European companies became involved in competition over their respective spheres of influence. This indirectly resulted in the dissolution of the Mughal empire. The British and the French, the stronger of the four, were already engaged in power struggles in Europe, which extended to India. Ultimately, the British won and retained their ascendancy for the next two centuries.

The British first established a foothold in Bengal by defeating Siraj-ud-Daulah in the battle of Plassey in 1757, and not long afterwards trounced Mir Qasim in 1765. It was the beginning of what a Bengali poet described as 'a night of eternal gloom for India'. These two victories sealed the fate of the British in the country as they now had economic control over the people. The introduction of the Permanent Settlement entitled them to a substantial portion of the state revenues, which set up a system of feudal aristocracy. The peasants became poorer as their landlords pressed them for greater output to meet the demands of the British for greater and greater income. In time the British, bloated with their achievements in Bengal, extended their influence to other territories as well. Soon their economic supremacy translated itself to political supremacy.

The few uprisings against British dominance that took place at this time were local and sporadic. The Sepoy Mutiny in 1857 was the first organised revolt of its kind. The immediate catalyst was a rumour that pig and cow fat was being used to grease the cartridges that were supplied to the Indian troops. This offended both Hindu and Muslim religious sentiments. The first incident was at Meerut, from where it quickly spread to other areas in north and central India. The last surviving emperor of the Mughal dynasty, Bahadur Shah Zafar, was made the token leader. But the movement did not have nationwide support and lacked the organisational strength of the British, who were able to crush it easily. The emperor was exiled to Burma, where he died a broken and disillusioned man. In the meantime, no effort was being spared to strengthen British rule within the country to keep in check the rising tide of rebellion.

The revolt of 1857, which forced the British to introduce drastic changes to safeguard their imperial authority in the country, is considered a turning point in Indian history.

Power was transferred from the East India Company to the British Crown by an Act of Parliament in 1858, and in 1877 Queen Victoria was declared 'Empress of India'. Thus the Indian regions were placed under the direct control of the British Government, with the viceroy serving as the chief executive. The army was reorganised and the number of its British officers was increased. The princes who supported the British during the revolt were rewarded, thus ensuring a loyal but subordinate band of supporters of the British Raj. In return, the British promised never to annex their territories.

Not surprisingly, a number of questions on British dominance of India are frequently the subject of debate. How did it affect the nation? Was British rule one of exploitation without consideration for the sentiments and feelings of the people they colonised? Were the economics of trade always in favour of the white people from across the ocean? These and other questions if answered unequivocally in the affirmative would not recognise the many benefits the country did accrue from their presence.

Though the British policy of growing rich at the expense of the colonies resulted in economic drain and political exploitation, it had many advantageous side-effects. In order to increase British dominance and to transport raw materials to port towns for export, railways and telegraphs were established. This helped in reaching out to even the remotest of places. Along with the growth of communications, the setting up of universities, colleges and industries (particularly iron and steel), and the entry of Indians into the civil services could not but have obvious beneficial consequences. Social reforms against the practice of sati, the exploitation of women, child marriage and the stigma on widow remarriage aided social progress.

The 'Brahmo Samaj' in Bengal and the 'Arya Samaj' in the north were part of the social reform movement that gained prominence at the end of the 19th century and helped raise social consciousness against the evils of Hinduism. With the birth of the educated middle class and the intellectual awakening in the country came the beginnings of nationalism. Encouraged by A.O. Hume, a retired English civil servant, the Indian National Congress was formed in 1885 at a gathering of educated Indians in Bombay. While this Congress was initially visualised more as a 'safety valve' for the growing resentment at the British, its nature changed when its membership was thrown open to all. The moderates and the extremists agreed on freedom from British rule as their goal but differed on their tactics for its attainment. The extremists wanted absolute freedom—'here and now'—while the moderates were happy with reforms within the confines of British law and government. However, they did not represent the masses, and as a small group from the educated middle class, they were not able to shake off imperial control on their own.

Mass support for the nationalist cause came with two notable events in the early 20th century. The first was the partition of Bengal into two provinces by the British in 1905, and the second was the arrival of Mohandas Karamchand Gandhi from South Africa in 1917. The partition was seen as an attempt to divide and rule, though the British held that it was an administrative decision. Protest marches, meetings and hunger strikes took place in Bengal. Bengal was the starting point of protests where the common person was included. This mass involvement which spread to other areas was organised into a national movement, by M.K. Gandhi, to weaken the stronghold of the British.

Gandhi launched the non-cooperation movement and the boycott of British goods which brought the entire British administration to a halt even though it was entirely peaceful. The perplexed British retaliated by banning meetings. But this sparked off mass protests like the one in Amritsar, which led to the Jallianwala Bagh massacre of innocent crowds in 1919. It became increasingly clear that 'Home Rule' was not sufficient and the cries of people demanding complete independence grew progressively shrill and persistent. The 'Quit India Movement' of 1942 forced the British to start conferences with the Indians to grant them freedom at the end of the Second World War.

Finally, India gained Independence on 15 August 1947. But freedom was not without a price. The British, during their time, had encouraged divisions between the Hindus and Muslims which led to the formation of the Muslim League in 1906. With partition, the Muslim League, governed by sectarian Muslim politics, struck out to establish its own identity and the nation was divided into two countries: India and Pakistan.

SOME REGIONS, CITIES AND TOWNS OF INDIA

Every city has its own special characteristics but is simultaneously a microcosm of the country at large, reflecting its many contradictions. Foreigners first notice the glaring gap between the rich and the poor and then the strange juxtaposition of modern amenities with things which have stayed the same since time immemorial. A case in point is the coexistence of the bullock cart and the most 'high-tech' computer in modern India.

Bombay, the Financial and Commercial Capital of India

Bombay is the 'gateway to India'. With an estimated 2,000 people coming to this 'El Dorado' every day to swell its existing population of thirteen million, it is the largest city in India. It is also the commercial capital, where fortunes are made and unmade in one day through the skulduggery and rags-to-riches success stories of its smugglers and film stars. Both the underworld and the film industry are strongly entrenched here. The city does not have a distinct regional character because of its mixed population. This also makes it very cosmopolitan. Being an island, it has space only for upward expansion and has also been described both as the 'Hollywood' ('Bollywood' in common parlance) and 'Manhattan' of India.

The island of Bom Bain (Good Bay) was given as part of the bride's dowry to King Charles of England when he married the Portuguese princess, Catherine of Braganza, in 1662. A few years later, it was leased to the East India Company. The city grew in importance with the opening of the railways in the mid-19th century, and its natural harbour became an international port of call with the building of the Suez Canal in 1869. Bombay soon eclipsed Calcutta as a port and as the financial capital of India. Calcutta was further marginalised when the British officially recognised Delhi as the seat of government and transferred the capital from Calcutta to Delhi in 1912. Though Delhi continued to be the bureaucratic centre of government, it was Bombay which attracted national and international capital and commerce.

Bombay is home to people of different communities. Maharashtrians and Gujaratis form a substantial part of the city's population. The small but strong group of Parsis, who originally came from Iran to India for commerce, have been greatly responsible for the development of Indian industry. Jamshed Tata established textile mills and set up the steel city of Jamshedpur; J.R.D. Tata pioneered the growth of the Indian airline industry. The Tata group has since diversified into other fruitful ventures and is a name easily recognised at home and abroad. Beside the small but ancient minority of Jews—mostly doctors, teachers, nurses and lawyers—there are the Christians from the neighbouring state of Goa who are engaged in teaching, trade and commerce. The separate identity each community maintains has given rise to a mix of places of worship, customs and rituals, which is evident everywhere.

The influence of the intermingling of different cultures is also to be noted in the architecture of the city. Unlike north India, where the ancient ruins of Mughal and Hindu dynasties are to be found everywhere, Bombay was founded and grew as a British city with fine churches and public buildings. It is the British landmarks which stand out in Bombay; though post-colonial buildings like hotels, hospitals and skyscrapers also dominate the landscape. The British, on the other hand, constructed imposing buildings at strategic points to show off their imperial power.

Examples of colonial architecture are the Old Secretariat, the Municipal Building, the University Hall, Elphinstone College, the School of Art, Crawford Market, Flora Fountain, the Prince of Wales Museum, St. George's Hospital, Victoria Terminus, Central Railway and the Gateway of India; of which the last mentioned is the most famous. Designed by the British architect, George Wittet, it was built as a memorial to King George's visit to the Delhi Durbar with Queen Mary in 1911, when the capital was shifted from Calcutta to Delhi. Ironically, it was through this arch that the last of the British troops in India left by sea in 1948.

More than the architecture, it is the sea which surrounds the city on three sides that dominates the cultural consciousness of the city and dictates its lifestyles. Beaches and seaside promenades like Marine Drive, Chowpatti and Juhu beach, and the outlying resorts of Madh island, Marve, Manori and Gorai, though eaten into by the spread of urban expansion, are still the visitor's joy.

Bombay is also the departure point for the Elephanta Caves, an hour away by motor launch. Hailing back to the Rashtrakuta dynasty, this is a series of beautiful rock-cut caves with temples and sculptures, including the six-metre, three-headed bust of Shiva in his three manifestations as Creator, Preserver and Destroyer. The caves were named by the Portuguese after the massive elephant structure that once stood here, which has since been shifted to the Bombay zoo.

Aurangabad

Named after Aurangzeb, who made this town a base for his expansion in the Deccan, Aurangabad is known for its monuments like the Bibi-Ka-Muqbara, a poor imitation of the Taj Mahal. The Daulatabad fort and Aurangzeb's burial spot are not far away, but as places of interest they are overshadowed by the Ajanta and Ellora caves nearby.

Ajanta

There are around thirty caves on the Deccan plateau which were excavated in different periods between 200 BC and AD 600. Situated in a secluded site in the hills three hours away from Aurangabad, they were forgotten until they were accidentally discovered in the 19th century. Luckily, down the centuries, they escaped defacement from marauding invaders. The caves look magnificent from the approach road which winds its way through sunflower and cotton fields, set against a backdrop of high, lush green hills and waterfalls (especially true during the monsoon season).

In the early centuries following the Buddha's teachings, he was represented by symbols and other images. Buddha was against idol-worship and his followers were forbidden from making images of him. He did not like the idea of colourful garments or any other form of ornamentation which might provoke desire. The later Mahayana sect began to erect graceful images of the Buddha to adorn stupas and Chaitya prayer halls. The Ajanta caves, while adhering to the basic philosophy, do not follow the Buddhist tenet of self-denial and the negation of the senses. In fact, the frescoes and sculptures are full of colourful imagery. Buddha's previous incarnations and tales from the 'Jataka' describing incidents from his life are depicted here. The caves numbered 1, 2, 9, 10, 16, 17, 19, 21 and 26 are the most important.

Ellora

About thirty kilometres from Aurangabad and close to the fort of Daulatabad, lie the Ellora caves which were excavated between the 6th and 11th centuries. Their magnificence lies in the fact that as much as 70,000 square metres of solid rock have been chiselled out of a mountain to make the centrepiece—the monolithic Kailash Temple, thirty metres high. Built by the Rastrakutas, the style shows interesting similarities to the Kailashnath Temple at Kanchipuram and the Chalukya temple at Pattadakal. Of the countless panels based on Hindu mythological themes on the outside walls of the temple, a particularly inspiring one shows Shiva and Parvati against Ravana, which symbolically represents the fight between the forces of good and evil.

Ellora differs from the entirely Buddhist sculptures of Ajanta in that it is a mix of Buddhist, Jain and Hindu monuments excavated and sculpted during different epochs.

Rajasthan

Though most of this state in western India lies in the desert, the beauty of its palaces, forts, colourfully dressed people, and camels and elephants, make it a popular tourist spot. The Rajputs, who were mostly warriors, have a proud history. Being a frontier state which also lay on the trade route to the west, Rajasthan bore the brunt of invasions by foreigners. Hence forts, or at least self-contained villages, were built strategically for defence. Merchant houses and havelis in the towns also looked inward on to one or more court-yards. Today, they create an atmosphere of romance and adventure. Beside the more frequently visited Udaipur and the capital, Jaipur, the two desert towns of Jaisalmer, built of pleasantly-coloured sandstone, and Jodhpur, slightly off the beaten track, have a charm so typical of this enchanting state. An hour's drive from Jaipur is the Samodh Palace, a fort with inbuilt facilities. Bikaner, which has many palaces designed by Sir Jacob Swinton, is to the north of Jaipur.

Udaipur

Udaipur is the greenest of the cities of Rajasthan and is also known as the 'city of lakes'. It has a rich history of resistance to the Mughals. The surrounding areas of Haldi Ghati and Chittor bear testimony to the fierce battles between the Rajputs and the Mughals. The legends of Rana Sangh and Rana Pratap are still sung by the people of the area. The long and turbulent history of the Rajputs also includes defiance of the British. As late as 1911 when the Delhi Durbar was held to honour George V, the only empty chair belonged to Maharana Fateh Singhji, whose displeasure at British rule was well known. The chair which signified the Rajput sense of pride is still on display at the City Palace. The Maharanas of Mewar can trace their family to Bapa Rawal of 728, while the history of Jodhpur and Jaipur follows by 483 and 400 years respectively.

Udaipur is most famous for its Lake Palace, in the middle of Lake Pichola. Once upon a time, it used to be a royal summer retreat. It has now been converted into a luxury hotel. This holiday resort looks especially beautiful in the monsoons, when the lake is full and overflowing. The City Palace, the residence of the Maharana of Udaipur, is at the other end of the lake. The older part of the palace has been made into a museum which contains the largest collection of Mewari paintings, while another section is now the Shiv Niwas Palace, a luxury hotel.

Ranakpur: Situated about 98 kilometres from Udaipur, Ranakpur has magnificent Jain temples belonging to the mid-15th century. The Rishabji temple with its 1,444 carved columns, of which no two are alike, and the Sun Temple nearby, are particularly notable. It is an important pilgrim centre for Jains.

Jaipur

Jaipur was founded by Dule Raja, the handsome warrior prince of the Kachhwaha dynasty, in 1128. For centuries this warrior caste protected the frontiers of the country. However, it was not until the twenty-second Maharaja, Raja Jai Singh, ascended the throne, six centuries later, that the present city of Jaipur was built.

Raja Jai Singh planned the city as we know it today. He enlisted the help of an artist from Bengal and separated the city into nine blocks, which were further divided into 107 sub-blocks in what was perhaps the first attempt at urban development proper.

Besides being an able ruler, he is best remembered for his interest in astrology. He built five observatories in the country to survey the movements of heavenly bodies and a thirty-metre-high sundial that indicated the hour when the sun's shadow moved every four metres, to gauge the time of day. Another achievement was an instrument that measured planetary and astral positions in the universe.

Jaipur is a city of monuments of which the Hawa Mahal, with its rosy facade and intricately patterned balconies, is a tourist landmark. It was built in 1799 by Raja Ram Singh so that his queens and concubines could watch—unobserved—royal processions that passed by in the street below.

City Palace: The official residence of the Maharajas of Jaipur is the City Palace. It was partly converted into a museum in 1959 and houses many royal treasures. One of the two main objects of interest is the two-metre-wide pajamas and two and a half-metre-long tunic that once clothed Raja Madho Singh, a heavy man of 250 kilogrammes.

The other major attraction is the Diwan-e-Khas in which is exhibited huge silver jars, each 350 kilogrammes in weight—the largest in the world. There is an interesting story about them that speaks of the religious sentiments of 19th- and early 20th-century Hindus. When the Maharaja was invited to the coronation of King Edward VII, a luxury liner was chartered and outfitted to suit his royal tastes. As a measure against stepping on impure, alien land on his arrival, sand from Jaipur was put inside his shoes and the silver jars were filled with the holy waters of the Ganges so that the Maharaja could purify himself at all times. Also, silver and gold offerings were made to the sea to ward off evil spirits. The silver jars, therefore, symbolise the King's compromise that enabled him to travel overseas and yet remain pure.

The nearby Diwan-e-Am contains beautifully illustrated manuscripts preserved under glass covers and numerous carpets that once adorned the palace walls.

The present Maharaja, 'Bubbles' to his friends, resides with his wife and daughter in their private apartments in Chandra Mahal.

Rambagh Palace: In the 18th century, the Rambagh Palace was the hunting lodge of Maharaja Ram Singh. It was later converted into a royal guest house. Raja Madho Singh II, who had then ascended the throne, instructed Sir Jacob Swinton to refurbish it. Maharaja Swai Man Singh II—'Jai'—decided to make it his residence in the 1930s. He lived here with his three wives; his third, Maharani Gayatri Devi, the princess of Coochbehar, was just thirteen years old when they fell in love. They were married in 1940. After he died in England in 1970 during a polo game, the Maharani then moved to the Lily Pool behind the palace, where she still lives. Her son lives in Moti Doongri, a lovely castle nearby.

Amber Palace: The Amber Palace, eleven kilometres north of Jaipur, comes into view around the last bend in the winding road. Built by Mughal architects during the reign of Man Singh I in the 16th century, the palace is set amid the charming Aravalli hills. It boasts paintings and marble panels set in relief by artists of the Mughal court. Of particular beauty is the art of mirror inlay-work in wet plaster which would reflect a thousand stars against the ceiling if a single flame was lit in the room.

A leisurely ride up to the fort by elephant offers a panoramic view of the city and its many other forts. All in all, it is an unforgettable experience for any visitor.

Within the fort is the Kali Mata Temple, where the image of the goddess was brought from Jessor in Bengal and installed here by Man Singh I in 1604. The temple is made of marble of different colours and has a silver door which depicts the Goddess Kali in her many forms of feminine energy.

The older Jaigarh Fort, the fabled storehouse of royal treasure, commands the ridge above the palace. The biggest cannon in the country, from which a single shot has never been fired, is to be found here.

Shopping in Jaipur: Jaipur is well known for its organised bazaars which their founder, Jai Singh, had planned. He wanted the city to be recognised for its elaborate artistry and fine craftsmanship. His wish is alive today in the dazzling array of emeralds, rubies and brassware that can be found in various pockets in the city. The splendour of the Maharaja's jewellery is on display at the Gem Palace.

Delhi, the Capital of India

It is often said that the history of India is the history of Delhi. New Delhi, the capital of India, has always occupied a strategic position in the country's history as different Hindu and Islamic dynasties have ruled from here, leaving their imprint in the form of relics which recapture those bygone times. Its history goes back to the days of the Mahabharata, when the Pandavas lived on the banks of the river Yamuna. Their kingdom, near Indraprastha, has been identified as Delhi. Indraprastha later became Dhillika, the first of the seven medieval cities of Delhi. Its significant location, about 1,000 kilometres from the Khyber Pass (the entrance point for most foreign invaders) increased its importance as a vital strategic position in the defence of the country.

Qila Rai Pithora, the first known city of Prithviraj Chauhan III, was taken over by Mohammed Ghori. Qutub-ud-Din Aibak, who succeeded him to the throne after his death, made Delhi his capital in 1192. As these foreigners made the newly conquered lands their home, they gradually began to incorporate the Indian way in their lifestyles, thereby evolving a whole new culture. These influences are most evident in Indo-Islamic architecture which reflects the cultural synthesis that has taken place in Delhi over the centuries. An example of this unique style is found in the Quwat-ul-Islam mosque, where the arches have an Islamic style with floral pillars and fine calligraphy, while the columns are similar to those in Hindu and Jain temples.

The Khalji Sultanate, which came to power in 1290 after toppling the Sultans, raised the second Delhi township of Siri, northeast of the Qila. The Tughluqs who ruled after the Khaljis, built the third city of Tughluqabad to the extreme south of Delhi; and then the cities of Jahanpanah and Firozabad on the banks of the river Yamuna. When the Mughals replaced the Tughluq dynasty in the early 16th century, its founder, Babur, concentrated on developing Agra and made it his capital. But his son, Humayun, constructed a new capital on the banks of the river Yamuna around the ancient capital of Indraprastha, a little south of Firozabad, and called it Din Panah. He also built a citadel, the Purana Qila. Shah Jahan, successor to Jahangir, created Shahjahanabad along the river as the well planned, seventh township of Delhi. It remained the Mughal capital until 1857, despite the decline of the Mughal Empire since 1707. A monument that remains a proud reminder of their rule is the majestic Red Fort.

Delhi after 1857: In 1857, when the British Crown took over the running of India from the East India Company, the viceroy and the government were at Calcutta, the then commercial capital because of its access to the tea gardens and coal fields. However, in 1911, the decision was made to establish a new capital at Delhi which was more centrally located. Plans were made to build a new city to befit the 'Jewel in the British Crown'. The area along the ridge, south of Shahjahanabad, was chosen as the site for the imperial capital. It was built on a regal scale by January 1931. Though the city has grown enormously subsequent to Independence in 1947, it is this area that boasts many of the best landmarks bequeathed by the British.

Lutyens and Baker designed much of the red sandstone architecture along the stretch between India Gate at one end and Rastrapathi Bhawan (the President's residence) at the other; with the adjoining administrative buildings of North Block and South Block, Parliament House and Connaught Place nearby. A number of other equally imposing complexes have come up in this area, which is still the administrative and commercial centre of the city.

For all its imposing presence, 20th-century British architecture pales in significance when compared with the relics of dynasties gone before. The historical ruins and monuments of former empires in Delhi may be divided into pre-Islamic and Indo-Islamic architecture for convenience.

The Rock Edict of the Buddhist emperor Ashoka (273—236 BC) in south Delhi, the best known of pre-Islamic relics, bears the inscription of the great emperor's appeal to follow the path of peace and righteousness. A similar call to the people is expressed in the writings on two pillars, one of which is located in Feroz Shah Kotla, whilst the other stands in

The small tomb of Mirza Ghayas Beg, who was the father of Jahangir's beloved consort, Nur Jahan, is called Itimad-ud-Daulah (pillar of stone) and lies across the river from the Agra Fort. Nur Jahan used her influence with the emperor to make her father the prime minister, and later had him buried in the same sepulchre that enshrined the remains of Shah Jahan's grandparents. The Itimad-ud-Daulah, often described as the 'baby Taj', looks like a jewel box from a distance.

Fatehpur Sikri: About fifty kilometres west of Agra lies the ghost town of Fatehpur Sikri with its red sandstone mansions. It was built to honour the Sufi saint, Salim Chishti, who had predicted the Mughal emperor Akbar would have three sons. Fatehpur Sikri took six years to build under the personal supervision of Akbar, who made it his capital for twelve years. But the city was later abandoned and the capital moved to Lahore.

Fortunately, the buildings are remarkably well preserved, probably because of the dry climate. The Badgir Mahal (terraces) and the Diwan-e-Am (hall of public audience) are of considerable significance. The red sandstone, quarried locally, gives the place a certain stability and exudes an architectural style quite unlike any in India, which combines an appreciation of the Hindu form with the outside influences of Central Asia and Iran. While the architecture of the saint's tomb, the monumental portals of Buland Darwaza and the pillared hall of the Jama Masjid complex show touches of Central Asia, the cloistered Diwan-e-Am and Diwan-e-Khas distinctly reveal their Turkish origins.

The tomb of St. Salim Chisti is revered by Muslims, and many thousands of devotees pilgrimage here every day to offer prayer requests.

Khajuraho

The tranquil town of Khajuraho, in the central Indian State of Madhya Pradesh, has the best medieval temples in India, well-known for their erotic sculptures. However, these form only a small part of the total, and the rest mostly depict the daily lives of the 10th and 11th-century people, from the ordinary to the royal court.

There used to be eighty-five temples in all, but only twenty-two survive today. Constructed in the Indo-Aryan style by the warrior clan of Chandelas, they were deserted with the advent of Islam. The site lay in disuse and was forgotten for eight centuries until 1838, when a British engineer rediscovered them. Their restoration took place through the patronage of the kings of nearby Chattarpur and Panna along with the help of the Archaeological Survey of India. Today they enjoy international fame.

The statues of gods and goddesses, warriors, celestial dancers or apsaras and animals are exceedingly elaborate but the erotic set of sculptures of couples in every conceivable sexual position called mithuna has been the focus of attraction. Some of the poses depicted are so complicated that they are possible only with the assistance of attendants. The Hindu philosophy of yoga and bhoga (physical pleasure), the two paths that lead to final liberation (moksha) is the underlying theme of these sculptures.

The best preserved temple is the Lakshmana Temple with its four subsidiary shrines. A candle kept aflame in front of the central statue gives a celestial aura to the rest of the temple. It is a treat to watch it at dawn when the sun's rays first kiss Lord Vishnu's feet before lighting up the whole statue.

The tallest temple, the Kandariya Mahadev, is dedicated to Lord Shiva and has a shikara (spire) which is thirty-eight metres high. Of its many statues, the most interesting is the one of a yogi performing the shirsh asan (headstand while having intercourse with three women at the same time). The statues are a window to the Indian concept of feminine beauty — large eyes, big breasts and swelling hips.

The best time in the year to visit Khajuraho is March when the leading dancers of the country perform against the backdrop of the Kandariya Mahadev Temple, in a replay of what must have happened centuries ago when temple dancers used to entertain the gods.

Varanasi

Varanasi, or Kashi (City of Light), is an ancient town that sits on the left bank of the river Ganges in Uttar Pradesh. It is known for its temples and bathing ghats (steps leading from the bank into the river). This holy site dates back to the first millennium BC. Since that time it has been a great centre of learning and culture, and still retains the traditional way of life despite the inevitable spread of urban development. The main temples here are the Vishwanath Temple, Durga Kund, Sankat Mochan, Annapurna and Kal Bairawa.

Temples

Varanasi ranks among the holiest of Hindu pilgrim centres as Lord Shiva's trident is believed to be the foundation on which the whole city rests. All devout Hindus wish to die in Kashi as this is said to ensure moksha from the cycle of birth and rebirth. As this is not always possible, most expect at least to be cremated here. Cremation takes place all through the night and day, and the river banks are well tamped down by the endless cavalcade of tightly bound corpses. The earth of Manikaran Ghat, which is the busiest, is said to be permanently hot. As one last alternative to death or cremation at Kashi, the devout Hindu undertakes a pilgrimage here to purify the soul, at least once in a lifetime. It is therefore not surprising that only a little over half the population is permanently resident here. The rest is composed of an endless stream of pilgrims.

Aside from its temples, Kashi is also famous for the lovely Banarasi silk saris of intricate and colourful weaves that most Indian women include in their wedding trousseaux. Its paan, a betel leaf envelope enclosing a mixture of arecanut, cardamom and lime, which Indians chew habitually, is also well known. A special variety of mango is also much sought after.

Sarnath

The Buddhist centre of Sarnath, where Gautam Buddha delivered his first sermon after attaining enlightenment, is ten kilometres north of Varanasi. Though repeated Muslim invasions ruined many of the structures that represented the Buddhist influence of the time, an Ashokan pillar—the main shrine—and the Dhamekh Stupa are still intact. The local archaeological museum, which has recovered specimens that stretch across a period of 1,500 years, houses a seated Buddha of the 6th century and Ashoka's lion capital belonging to the 3rd century BC. The lion capital has since been adopted as the national emblem.

South India

South India, bounded by the Indian Ocean in the south, by the Bay of Bengal in the east, and by the Arabian Sea in the west, is largely comprised of the four Dravidian states of

Kerala, Karnataka, Andhra Pradesh and Tamil Nadu (in India, language has been the overriding criterion for the division of states). Though they are treated as a unit for convenience, and share certain basic similarities in outlook to the undiscerning visitor, they have distinct cultural and linguistic traditions. What we know as south India does not necessarily conform to the location of the Tropic of Cancer, which runs through India and splits the country into two equal halves.

However, the Hindus here share a common preference for Murugan, Durga, Ganesha, Shiva and Vishnu among the innumerable gods in the Hindu pantheon. Islam is predominant mostly in Hyderabad in Andhra Pradesh, where the Mughals had tried briefly to make inroads into the Deccan, and in some parts of coastal Kerala, the southernmost state, which used to be thriving centres of commerce for seafaring Arab traders in the 15th and 16th centuries. Kerala also had a strong Christian influence and was a base for missionary work. Hence, some of the largest concentrations of Christians in India are to be found here.

Tamil Nadu

Madras, the fourth largest metropolis after Calcutta, Bombay and Delhi, is the capital of Tamil Nadu and is also known as the 'gateway to the south'. Large numbers of the original Tamil population have migrated to countries like Burma, Sri Lanka, Australia and the Far East. Consequently, Madras is well connected with these countries. The city is also linked by air, train and bus with the rest of India.

Madras is an odd mixture of cultures where the influences of the British East India Company coexist with traditional Tamil culture, with its flourishing motion picture industry. Therefore, it is not uncommon to find huge old colonial bungalows and churchyards jostling with temples and gigantic cinema hoardings for space and attention.

British Madras: The British legacy predominates in the colonial architecture of the administrative buildings in Madras, especially Fort St. George, the Tamil Secretariat and the Legislative Assembly. A number of other buildings of the period lie within Fort St. George, including the Fort St. George Museum with its exhibits brought together by the East India Company and during the Raj. St. Mary's Church, also within the complex, was consecrated in 1680 and is the oldest Anglican church in the East. Elihu Yale, founder of Yale University in the U.S.A., was connected with it; as was Robert Clive (believed to be responsible for establishing the British Empire in India by winning the battle of Plassey in 1759), who was married here.

Of the various churches in Madras, St. George's Cathedral and St. Andrew's Kirk, both of which were consecrated in the 19th century, deserve mention. The San Thome Church on the Main Beach Road is perched on St. Thomas' Mount, and is associated with Christ's apostle, Thomas. The Christian influence is equally evident elsewhere in the state, particularly in Kodaikanal and Ootacamund, two much frequented hill stations in the south.

South India is famed for its temples around which entire townships have sprung up. Unlike in the north, the temple in the south has not confined itself to being merely a place of worship but is responsible for setting moral standards and establishing village assemblies, tribunals, banks, granaries, hospitals and schools around it, thereby serving as the custodian of society. This reflects in the conservative mores of the people, and probably explains why the temples are often in the very heart of the city.

The Dravidian influence in temple architecture and art has been strong in the south due to the relatively small role played by the Aryans. Each temple complex is a walled enclosure (prakarama) of concentric walls and corridors that houses markets, workshops, educational centres and living quarters. Every temple has towers (gopurams) that face the four cardinal points of the compass and serve as landmarks for travellers. Features that are associated with the temple itself include the water tank and flower garden, and a temple chariot that is drawn through the streets on festival days by hundreds of devotees with the deity mounted on it.

Many temples in south India are made of red sandstone and have sculptures carved out of niches and walls in bold relief. Sculptures of granite which have been worked separately and then set in niches are also a common feature of granite temples in Tamil Nadu.

Temple Tours

The temple tours of Tamil Nadu cover places like Tiruchirupalli, Mahaballipuram, Kanchipuram, Madurai, Thanjavur, and Rameshwaram, among others, and all of them start from Madras.

Mahaballipuram: Mahaballipuram, which was the port city of the Pallavas, the ruling dynasty of the 7th century, is situated thirty kilometres from Madras. Temple architecture elsewhere in the south has been greatly inspired by its finely sculptured, rock-cut monoliths (seventy in number) of which the most notable are the five rathas carved after classical Indian epic heroes.

Tiruchirupalli: The Ranganatha Temple, built by the Cholas and improved upon by subsequent dynasties, stands in the middle of the river Kaveri on an island which is close to Tiruchirupalli. It has the distinction of being the most complex of south Indian temples and its evening ceremony is especially worth a visit.

Kanchipuram: Kanchipuram, seventy kilometres from Madras, is known as the 'City of a Thousand Temples' and boasts, among others, the Kailashnatha Temple, dating from 725 and the Vishnu Temple, dating back to 750. Both are known for their beautiful statues of Nataraja, Vishnu, Shiva and Durga. The broad streets of this capital city of the Cholas and the Pallavas, two prominent south Indian dynasties, have been designed to contain crowds during the festivals of the many deities worshipped here.

Thanjavur: Thanjavur contains many elegant temples, of which the tallest ancient monument in India is the Brihadeshvara Temple, which rises to a height of over ninety-one metres over thirteen floors in stark pyramid form, with its ground floor raised on two levels.

Madurai: A worthwhile stopover would be at the Meenakshi Temple in Madurai which, besides housing a museum of exquisite statues in its hall of a thousand pillars, epitomizes a south Indian temple town, complete with a complex of walls, corridors, concentric streets, tanks and shops which eventually lead to the main shrine.

Rameshwaram: At the southern tip of India is the Ramanathaswamy Temple in Rameshwaram, an important pilgrim centre for Hindus. The world's largest pillared and cloistered corridor, two kilometres in length, is an integral architectural feature of this temple.

Kerala

Kerala, the land of coconut and spice, is also the greenest state in the country with its backwaters and palm trees. The people of Kerala are a harmonious mixture of Hindu, Muslim and Christian communities. It is reputed for what are probably the most exciting snake boat races in the world, conducted during the Onam festival. Chinese fishing nets, Dutch palaces, the oldest synagogue in Asia, and elegant Kathakali dancers are other compelling features of this state.

Karnataka

Bangalore: Bangalore is the capital of Karnataka and, after Bombay, is India's most cosmopolitan city. Its rapid growth and development, especially in the field of electronics, has attracted a number of talented young professionals. However, the old-world charm of bygone days is not totally lost and pockets of the city still exude this flavour. The Legislative Building and Botanical Gardens are two places of particular note. The wealth of Karnataka, however, lies beyond the city limits.

Mysore: The former princely state of Mysore is famous for its sandalwood and jasmine gardens. The Mysore Palace is especially attractive during the Dussehra festival.

Temples of Karnataka: The Keshava Temple of Somnathpur, built on a star-shaped stone platform and supported by lathe-turned stone columns, exemplifies Hoysala architecture. The temples of Belur and Halebid also illustrate this form and were the work of the master sculptor, Jakanachari, who enjoyed the patronage of the ruler at that time, Vishnu Uadharma. The Hindu and Jain temples at Badami, carved out of the mountain, were built in the 6th century during the reign of King Pulakesin II.

The 8th century Chalukya rulers used their Pattadakal temples not only for worship but also for coronation ceremonies. Aihole, a centre for Hindu and Jain temples, is an interesting study in the development of architectural styles over six centuries, spanning the dynasties of the Chalukya and Rastrakuta rulers.

Shravenabelagola: The eighteen-metre-high monolithic statue of Bahubali, carved out of living rock atop the Udaygiri mountain, is the chief attraction at Shravenabelagola. It is an important pilgrimage centre in south India for Jains. Hampi, which was once the capital of the Vijayanagar empire, was reduced to ruins in the 16th century.

India as a travel destination has been a major attraction for centuries. Its many vibrant cultures and superb monuments embracing almost two thousand years of history are only part of the fascination the land holds for visitors. Its principal lure is the warmth of the people whose friendly smiles and eyes make every stranger feel very much at home.

A trip to India is a sure way to appreciate the diversity and richness of this vast land. Compare it with the many other lands around the globe and see how one country can offer the best of mountains, deserts, seas and jungles; beside a rich, exotic and varied canvas painted with scenes from an ancient culture. History, art, religion, language and custom make up the national fabric which is unique to India. And as the people beckon with neatly folded hands in the traditional welcoming—*namaste*—make your plans to explore further this fascinating land in what could well become one of the most valuable experiences of a lifetime.

Some of Bombay's most beautiful buildings were built by the British during their colonial rule. The Gateway of India on the seafront was built to commemorate the visit of King George and Queen Mary in 1911. Today, skyscrapers and high-rise buildings form the skyline of modern Bombay, proclaiming it a great cosmopolitan city.

Bombay's 19th-century British architecture was
inspired by Gothic churches and contemporary
European buildings. Even Victoria Terminus
still has an air of imperial grandeur.

Elephanta island is an hour's boat ride from the Gateway of India in Bombay. In the seventh century a huge temple was cut out of a rocky hillside on the island— rooms, pillars, shrines and monumental sculptured friezes were created out of rock. The temple is dedicated to Shiva, and an enormous trimurti (three-headed sculpture) at the back of the hall depicts this god as the Creator, Preserver and Destroyer of the universe.

Ajanta is a World Heritage site with over 30 Buddhist shrines and monasteries carved into the side of a cliff. Each carved monastery (vihara) and prayer hall (chaitya) was hewn out of the hill and decorated with sculptured friezes, and the walls and ceilings were painted with frescoes in vibrant mineral colours. The themes of the murals range from Buddhist legends or Jataka tales to decorative patterns of flowers and animals.

Ellora is a spectacular site with rock-cut caves made by Buddhist, Hindu and Jain communities between the sixth and ninth centuries A.D. It is about 30 km from the historic city of Aurangabad, built by Aurangzeb, the rebellious son of Shah Jahan. The most famous site at Ellora is Kailash, the great temple dedicated to Shiva. The temple was cut out of the hillside and is complete with shrines, halls and inner chambers decorated with sculptured panels. The artists began work from the top of the temple tower, cutting the temple from rock and carving the decorations simultaneously, leaving little margin for error.

Following Pages: Udiapur, the 'Sunrise City', was founded in the 16th century as the capital city of the Mewar Rajputs, the clan who ruled over this region of Rajasthan. It stands between two lakes, Pichola and Fateh Sagar. Lying amidst the tranquil waters of Lake Pichol is the spectacular Lake Palace, now a luxury hotel, while on the shores of the lake stands the City Palace, part of which has been opened so that the public can admire its frescoes, stone and glass mosaics, and ornamental doors and painted shutters.

Chittor was the traditional capital of the Mewar Rajputs before they moved to Udaipur. Built on top of a formidable plateau, the Chittorgargh Fort's gigantic walls protected it for centuries against invasions attempted by the sultans of Delhi. Its beautiful ruined palaces, temples and water reservoirs capture the turbulent history of this ancient kingdom.

Following pages: *Ranakpur, 98 km from Udaipur, has some of India's most spectacular temples, built in honour of Jain tirthankaras (teachers). These 15th-century temples are famous for their magnificent architecture and intricately carved white marble ceilings and pillars*

The Mehrangarh Fort in Jodhpur stands serenely overlooking the modern town below. It was established in the 15th century by Rao Jodha and encompasses richly decorated palaces and courtrooms. Just outside the ancient city stands the stately Umaid Bhavan palace building, named after its founder, Maharaj Umaid Singh. From Jodhpur one can venture out into the desert to the fortified city of Jaisalmer.

Jaisalmer Fort stands in the middle of the Thar desert. Constructed on a hilly plateau, this sandstone city is a labyrinth of cobbled streets, elaborately decorated havelis (residences) and sumptuous palaces. To keep the brilliant desert sunlight out and to cool the inner rooms, the houses were built with towers and multiple windows.

Jaipur was built in the early 18th century by Jai Singh, a passionate astronomer who designed the city's huge observatory. The city came to be known as the 'Pink City' when Raja Ram Singh decorated the entire capital in this welcoming colour for the visit of the Prince of Wales in 1876—the custom has been continued, by law, to this day. The City Palace is still the residence of the Maharaja, although part of it has been opened to the public as a museum exhibiting textiles, paintings, weapons, carpets, manuscripts and glassware.

The pink city of Jaipur is a thriving commercial centre with streets lined with shops selling exquisite printed fabrics, leather items, silver jewellery and precious gems. The Hawa Mahal (Palace of Wind),with hundreds of latticed windows to catch the faintest breezes, was designed so that women could watch processions and celebrations on the streets below without being seen.

The Albert Hall (below) *now houses the Central Museum in Jaipur.*

Amber was the royal capital of the Kachhwaha kings before the city of Jaipur was built. It is a breathtaking palace-fort complex built on a hillside overlooking a beautiful garden and lake. The palaces within it are airy and cool, and are surrounded by enclosed gardens with ornamental fountains and waterways. The private rooms of the princes are decorated with mirrors, precious stone inlay and mural paintings.

Delhi, the capital of India, is a modern city that incorporates several ancient towns and forts, with a history of habitation going back over 3,000 years. In the 16th century, the Mughal rulers established Delhi, Agra and Lahore as their triumvirate of capital cities.

The tomb of Humayun, the second Mughal emperor, was used as a prototype model for the Taj Mahal.

Following pages: *The Qutub Minar is the towering minaret of the first Muslim mosque to be built in Delhi in 1199 out of the remains of previous temples.*
Purana Qila (Old Fort) was built by Humayun.

Delhi was also the capital of the later Mughal ruler Shah Jahan, who built Shahjahanabad, now known as the Red Fort, in 1648. The fort has massive red sandstone walls that enclose gardens, public and private chambers and the royal mosque. Outside the Red Fort is the huge Jama Masjid, the Friday Mosque designed by Shah Jahan for community worship.

The centre of New Delhi, the imperial city chosen to be the capital of the British empire, was designed by two British architects, Sir Edwin Lutyens and Sir Herbert Baker, in a composite of Indian, European and Classical styles. The Viceroy's residence is now Rashtrapathi Bhawan, the home of the President of India, and is surrounded by government offices. On national holidays, this impressive edifice is illuminated and decorated, as enchanting as the numerous bazaars in Old Delhi.

Lying downstrean from Delhi, Agra was once the capital of the Mughal rulers. The Red Fort, built on the banks of the River Yamuna, was the fortified royal residence of the Mughals . Within the fort are a number of courtyards and lavishly deco-rated palaces built of marble and red sandstone. The exquisite marble tomb of Itimad-ud-Daulah stands across the river in a private garden. The entire marble structure is inlaid with pre-cious and semi-precious stone designs and motifs.

Taj Mahal in Agra is without doubt the most beautiful Mughal building, the pinnacle of Mughal artistry. Designed as a tomb for the empress Mumtaz Mahal, wife of Shah Jahan, it is enclosed in a garden amidst fountains and ornamental trees. Work started on this monument in 1634 and continued for almost 22 years. The tomb is encased in white marble which reftects the changing light of day and is decorated with flaw-less marble sculptures and inlaid designs of flowers and callig-raphy cut from precious gems.

87

Fatehpur Sikri and Sikandra (along with the Akbar tomb) are the finest examples of Indo-Islamic architecture. Akbar favoured the use of red sandstone and, in keeping with the Islamic tradition, the palaces and tombs had elaborate gardens full of ponds and flowers constructed around them.

Fatehpur Sikri is the 'City of Victory' built by Akbar, the third Mughal emperor. The grand Buland Darwaza, built to commemorate Akbar's conquest of Gujarat, is the gateway to an enormous mosque. Within the court-yard of the mosque is the tiny marble tomb of Salim Chisti, who predicted that Emperor Akbar would have several heirs. The tomb, which is still a site of pilgrim-mage by childless women, has some fine single stone marble screens.

90

Khajuraho was an ancient city of temples built by the
Chandela rulers of Central India in the 10th and 11th centuries. More than 20 temples - though legend claims there
were once 85 - were built within this city. The temples are
raised on high platforms reached by steps, and the buildings are covered with bands of exquisite sculptures of
mythical animals, deities, celestial creatures and the
famous erotic friezes.

Varanasi, or Banaras, is an ancient holy city built on the sacred burning ghats of the River Ganges. It is believed that human sins are washed away by the waters of the mighty river. Thousands of Hindu pilgrims flock to the city to bathe, offer prayers and cremate their dead so that the ashes can be carried to eternity by the holy waters.

Sarnath is a few kilometres outside the city of Varanasi and is an important pilgrimage centre for Buddhists. The stupas and monasteries here mark the spot where the Buddha came, over 2,500 years ago, to deliver his first sermon and where he established the first Buddhist religious order.

Orissa, an eastern state of India, is a land of temples and
an ancient cultural tradition. Bhubaneshwar, the capital
city, has over a hundred Hindu stone temples. The seaside
resort town of Puri has the famous temple dedicated to
Jagannath, which draws thousands of people for the Rath
(Chariot) festival each year. The great temple at Konarak is
designed like a chariot with galloping stone horses and
giant wheels for the sun god, Surya, who rides through the
heavens.

Karnataka is a southern Indian state with several ancient cities and temple towns. Badami (preceding pages), Aihole and Pattadakal are deserted sites with temples built along craggy cliffs. The exquisite and profusely decorated temples of Belur, Halebid and Somnathpur belong to the Hoysala period of the 12th and 13th centuries. Hampi was the ancient capital of the Vijayanagar rulers, a magnificent site with fortresses, palaces and temples set in a glorious landscape.

The 18 metre-high statue of Gomateshvara (Bahubali), sculpted in the 10th century, marks a famous Jain pilgrimage centre.

Mysore, with the palace of the Maharaj, continues to be the centre of cultural life in Karnataka.

Following pages: Tamil Nadu is also a land of great temples. The early temples of Mahaballipuram outside Madras are simple rock-cut models on which the later temple complexes of Thanjavur and Madurai were built. The southern Indian temple's most prominent feature is the towering gateway or gopuram covered with sculptural details that signals the presence of the shrine to approaching pilgrims. The Brihadeshvara Temple, Thanjavur, recreates the southern mystical mountain supporting the universe.

Kerala is a southwestern state in India and is fringed with beaches and fishing villages. Its ancient seaports, such as Cochin, the earliest European settlement in India, attracted traders from Europe, the Middle East and China. A small Jewish synagogue built by European Jews fleeing from the Inquisition and Chinese fishing nets in Cochin mark its colourful past.

(Top) *Landscape in South India.*
(Above) *Snake boat race, Kerala, South India.*
(Right) *Lush green paddy fields, South India.*

A landscape of diversity, India is home to a stunning vista of peoples and cultures

*Modern India has inherited a culture both regal and flamboyant—from combinations of
classical European architecture fused with Mughal motifs to the vibrant celebration of
ancient religious festivals.*

Distributed By
FAMOUS BOOK STORE
25, Janpath Hutment, Janpath,
New Delhi Ph. 3008215